TESTIFY

TESTIFY

poems

Douglas Manuel

Red Hen Press | *Pasadena, CA*

Book layout by Silvia Gomez

Library of Congress Cataloging-in-Publication Data

Names: Manuel, Doug, author.

Title: Testify : poems / Doug Manuel.

Description: First edition. | Pasadena, CA : Red Hen Press, 2017. |
   Includes bibliographical references.

Identifiers: LCCN 2016048427 | ISBN 9781597090452 (pbk. : alk. paper)

Classification: LCC PS3613.A5845 A6 2017 | DDC 811/.6—dc23

LC record available at https://lccn.loc.gov/2016048427

The National Endowment for the Arts, the Los Angeles County Arts Commission, the Dwight Stuart Youth Foundation, the Max Factor Family Foundation, the Pasadena Tournament of Roses Foundation, the Pasadena Arts & Culture Commission and the City of Pasadena Cultural Affairs Division, the City of Los Angeles Department of Cultural Affairs, the Audrey & Sydney Irmas Charitable Foundation, Sony Pictures Entertainment, Amazon Literary Partnership, and the Sherwood Foundation partially support Red Hen Press.

First Edition

Published by Red Hen Press

www.redhen.org

ACKNOWLEDGMENTS

I am especially grateful to these journals for publishing these poems or earlier versions of them: *The Chattahoochee Review*: "The Cripple and the Crackhead"; *Crab Creek Review*: "Fishing" and "I Can Run Five Miles but Can't Get to the Other Side of My Mind"; *Many Mountains Moving*: "Entreaties"; *New Orleans Review*: "Goodnight, Baby" and "Heading Down"; *North American Review*: "Washing Palms"; *Revolution John Magazine*: "All Is Laughter," "Baubles," and "Of Wasp Hum and Catacombs,"; and *Rhino*: "I'll Leave Your Ass Here."

For Mama, Aunt Yvette, and Kay,

my holy trinity

CONTENTS

I

II

III

I

LOUD LOOKS

You better rap, my brother
says—he can
b-box his ass off.
Got DJ scratches and spins,

will drop it on the two
and four, the three and four.
Whatever you need.

Me posing my bars: *My flows*
are second to none, come here,
son. See how it's done.

Wanted to be a rapper? Check.
Thought I was going to the NBA? Check.
Father went to prison? Check.
Brother too? Check.
Mother died when I was eight? Check.
Hung pictures of Luke Perry
on my bedroom wall?

What?

Yep, give me a bit, and I'll sprinkle
some subjectivity on it.

I loved that dude, his whisper-voice, his lean.
Auntie worried on the phone:
Girl, he got photos of some white boy

all over his walls. Me rocking out
to Tom Petty's "You Don't Know How It Feels."

Silent head nods do more
than throw shade.

All black people are fluent

in silence. Mangled Baldwin quote?
Let's keep wrenching. Everybody's

fluent in silence.

You know what
a switchblade glare means. No need
to read the look she gave me

as those white man's lyrics
flung out my mouth.

WASHING PALMS

When the junkies my father sold crack to got
too close to me, he told them to back up

six dicks' lengths. This is the man who when I was
seven caught me under the bed crying and said:

Save those tears. You'll need them later.
The man who told me he smoked crack

because he liked it, the man sitting on his couch
now watching the History Channel, scratching

the nub beneath his knee where his leg used to be,
gumming plums, his false teeth

soaking in vinegar on the table. I'm sitting
across the room trying to conjure each version

he's shown of himself, trying to lie
in water warm enough

to soak away the switch he hit me with.
To help me summon love for the man

who just asked me if he can borrow 200 dollars,
the man who once told me: *Wish*

in one hand, then shit in the other,
and see which one fills up the quickest.

AUBADE

I'm being watched
    by a gold timepiece,
tethered and swinging

from a belt loop
    on pleated khakis ironed
stiff as rigor mortis.

Red second hand
    tells me, *Don't worry.*
A woman waits

with a bare tit for your lips.
    Saying what I want to say
is like soothing the sun

with spit, like ladling out
    the bowels of an oak.
Shine tests my eyes. Flex

of heart. Air that's mine
    to catch. *Circle, circle,*
dot, dot. Nobody gave me

my shot. There must be
    a word, a phrase.
Break, voices! Interrupt.

A furnace churns
    downstairs. Cadavers
step out of my selves.

LITTLE FIRES LEFT BY TRAVELERS

The smoldering stops
me. I see my father in knee-deep
snow.
      Wet white sticks
to the blade. In Grandpa's snow
suit, dad is blue flame. Come
summer he'll be nude
under his overalls, yes, no

drawers, letting it hang and swang,
straight raw. Newport shaking
its red cherry. Smoke trailing
behind:
      something kind of like
the sparklers I used to write
my name with
         on the Fourth
of July, something not unlike

lightning bugs fighting night
with the shine of their asses.
Dad's shotgun bucking:
all strobe and flash.
        Can I get
a James Brown scream? Father's
legless, not Godless, charms the Lord
with his tongue, reads the red
words of Christ when I go.

GET YOUR HEAD OUT OF THE GUTTER

I want to dive inside, to graffiti
the walls of your mouth
so you'll never forget me, want to lay
a cobblestone road

     upon your tongue.

At St. Mary's,
teachers told us sex is
when a man loves a woman
so much he wants nothing

between them so he lies close
enough, inserts his—

     There, the bell
tower never knelled, not for weddings
or the going of the old. On a dare,
I climbed the stairs. A rope released

dust when I took hold
and pulled. I heard chimes,
felt rust fall into my eyes.

LUXURY ITEMS

A plastic bag.

Whim's wind.

No zipper like the ones they put bodies in. Suspended,

after flitting, after being
                    animate. A buoy,

easily ignored:
how many have I passed? What

did I need? Matches, rubbing
                    alcohol, razors?

So many things I would like to return:
                              fist I plunged

into my brother's gut, saliva
                    I hocked on his forehead

when he already had enough,
our mother
              dead on the cooling board.

Plastic bag, hard to observe,
impossible to ignore, waits
                    for a face.

AS IF I CAN UNCHISEL PAIN,

I stare at the statue

of a man stuck mid-crawl, right arm outstretched,

palm up as if begging,
hand cupped and empty. Is it

always empty? No, leaves and weeds,

rain and snow, shine and shadow
sometimes rest there. I have,
                            too many times,

left hands bare, ignored pleas,
turned my glare instead of looking. On his head,

a crow lands and stares.

FEELS LIKE RAIN

Dead black cat on the porch,

                        tongue out.

I touched it!

No regrets. I've told myself
for as long as I can forget.

                       I rode a Big Wheel

through snow, couldn't go back

as far as planned. *Manx cat, do you want a tail?*

Left too many blades under pillows. Band-Aids
never big enough. My father aches

in legs he doesn't have. That cat
was more his than mine.

                    He's like both of ours
only let's keep him at my house.

With a lit cigarette, I plugged an anthill.

BAUBLES

A crucifix hangs
in my skull.

Scriptures drip from my lips.
Choiceless,
            I caulk my mouth

to hold and save. Call them
coins, worth still

undetermined. Overhead,
a murder of crows, tar-babies

of God.
            Mother's eyes swirled,

showed only white
before she died.

Church mailed a Bible.

Gift and/or onus? It's in a box,
which resembles hers.

ENTREATIES

My brother promised me I was a God
and the world would end
on the first day of the 2g, said:

Little Doug, you need to be
on this real shit, this black shit,
this Five-Percent shit. When I asked

Grandma, she opened her Bible, moved
the red ribbon to the side, and placed
her long fingernail under David's pleas:

With a loud voice I cry out
to the Lord; with a loud voice
I beseech the Lord. My complaint

I pour out before him. I know
to close my eyes when holy words
are spoken. I do, and then it's 1989.

Trey has an Afro and a white jeep,
bricks of crack in the trunk. He's
rapping Rakim Allah to me: the god

MC limning mathematics, claims
of Egyptian blackness, rap tactics
of self-knowledge. Lyrical content, the only

words he said to me, hitting my chest
for emphasis at every dope line.
These niggas be telling the truth,

Little Doug, he would say. Grandma prayed,
prayed hard: *Dear Lord, seat of wisdom,*
mirror of justice, cause of our joy, please

have mercy on this boy and his brother.
Grandma died in November. Trey's back
in prison. I haven't prayed in years.

HEADING DOWN

We shouldn't raise mixed babies
in the South, Kay says as I drive up the crest
of another hill on our way into Kentucky.

The South, where humidity leaves
a sweat mustache, where a truck
with a Confederate flag painted

on the back windshield skitters in front
of us. In its bed, avoiding our eyes,
a boy with blond hair

split down the middle like a Bible
left open to the Book of Psalms.
His shirtless, sun-licked skin drapes,

a thin coat for his bones, his clavicles sharp.
I want to know who's driving this raggedy truck.
I want the boy to look at us. I want

to spray paint a black fist over that flag.
I want the truck to find its way
into the ravine. I want to—

Stepping on the gas, I pass the truck.
Kay and I turn our heads. The boy smiles
and waves. The man driving doesn't

turn his head, keeps his eyes on the road. Kay
turns red as she draws her fingers
into fists. I stare at the whites of her eyes.

ME, *THE BOONDOCKS*. HER, *SOUTH PARK*.

I hate Token. She can't stand
Uncle Ruckus. We watch reruns,
*Def Comedy Jam. The medium
is the message.* I have trouble
laughing until a man—*What's his nuts?*
An expression I stole from her—
says, *We all black when the lights go
out*: his rationale for fucking
white girls. Her mouth remains
shut, not the least tickled. Right
then, I knew we were a power drill
without a bit, lots of twerking,
no purpose. *All that is to come is
vanity.* Polar Vortex, 2010, white kids
ice skating to campus. Black ice
isn't black, just unseen. My car careened,
stuck for hours. She came
to get me. When Elijah Muhammad tried
to give Baldwin a name, James asked
for a ride to the white part of town. North
Side, Chi-town. Sixty-five stories high,
we peered down at Lake Michigan's
snow-water sheets fighting, colliding,
refusing to become solid ice.

INDEFENSIBLE

Honestly, I went to church camp for the girls.
Those youth group trips were the closest I'd ever get

to them. Holding hands to pray, crying as we passed
the candle and confessed our teenage evils. So much

lust but little of it had to do with the Lord.
The homies and I used to say, *She got a body on her.*

Meaning we found her attractive or that her body
was the only thing about her we liked. *Her face, man—*

We all memorized Pac's "Dear Mama"
and "Brenda's Got a Baby," but he's the same man

who gave us *All Eyez on Me.* Yep, "All Bout U"
and "Wonda Why They Call U Bitch." On the floor,

in the front room, playing chess, a female friend challenged
my love of hip-hop, called it sexist, asked what my dead

mother would think, talked about my brother
and father's prison bids. I didn't have the pocket cop-out

reply I have now: *Everything that's wrong with hip-hop
is the same shit that's wrong with America.* I put on

"Brown Skin Lady." I tried to get in more than a checkmate.

BEST ACT LIKE YOU KNOW

Corner of Nickel and Arrow,
marked by a stop sign, factories

and auto-plants gone, Bingo Halls
teeming like weeds, we share

a Newport. Trey's talking
about getting the *feet* on his car.

The Feet? I ask. *Rims, nigga,* he replies.
Two men approach, their fists

clenching bottle necks.
Trey lifts up his white shirt to expose

the Nine. *Just in case niggas trying
to clown,* he says. Gauging the distance

between my present and past is as hard
as trying to gouge out the eye of a fly.

Raw coke in a baggy. *Fools pleading
to hoop-score sentences for them rocks,*

he reports—*Doug Fresh, you will never
catch me slanging another fucking stone.*

BAD SON

Ghosts hang from hooks.
I don't know myself
in past pictures. In the Polaroid
days, I was a hi-top fade
and a lip-smile. Just lost
my two front teeth.
Didn't want who to see?
Probably me. Can't remember
what staring in the mirror
felt like then. Probably something
like taking off skates
and feeling shorter but stronger.
No, the present presses and mints
the past into a gold coin
you can't spend anywhere.
A savings account
with negative interest. Had dreads
in high school, wore almost
a pound of hemp. Sandals, my
shoes of choice. Amber
and shea butter, my smell.
Dad transferred
to Anderson's jail. More charges
pending. I didn't visit him.

MIC DROP

Grandma's grave remains unmarked. It was me
who was supposed to buy her headstone.

After finding out her plot was still uncrowned,
I promised.
                I promised to give dad my truck.
I promised to quit smoking, to say sorry more.

My apologies as bare as the stretch of land above her.
Promised I'd send my brother fifty dollars. Promised

I'd holla at my auntie at least once a month.
In the restlessness night gives,
                      I saw Mounds State Park,

the pavilion filled with every broken promise
congregating as though this was a church revival.

Mother and father both walking as though their legs
were never lost.
              Me at a podium, with a microphone:
I'm sorry. I am so sorry.
                My act of contrition
interrupted by voices. My past and future selves loudest

of all. They offer punishments: *Lashings? Guillotine?*
Electric chair? The noose? Banishment? Stones?

To get out of there I had to become Father Bob,
the holiest man I ever saw in flesh. Mirror to face,

I am him, aquiline nose, crow-claw eyebrows, skin
yellowed around eyes and joints.
                                        We do the magic trick

he always did. He pulls my thumb
off, and after a quick smoker's cough, puts it back.

I'LL LEAVE YOUR ASS HERE

Fuck you will, boy.

His steps, slow motion,
trail behind me, learning

to walk again. Two new prosthetic legs.
Six months ago he was all flat line

and moan. I wasn't there, didn't
go to the hospital, said I was too busy, was told

about him coding three times in one
night. I tell him, *Falling's not an option, Dad.*

His 250 pounds
too much: he'll always be more than

me. *Dougie, you ain't never
lied.* He's lying, always does, does

so much he doesn't even know it.
Once, we were walking.

Daddy, why the moon keep following me,
I asked, rushing to catch up. *Because you*

the only nigga who matter in the world.

II

"ARE YOU READY TO HELP THE PARENTS OF THIS CHILD IN THEIR DUTY AS CHRISTIAN PARENTS?"

My godmother answered *Yes* and traced
the sign of the cross on my forehead. I'm driving
to see her, pines blotching the side
of the road. I want Cindy to stay
young. She uses a walker now, an old woman,
curly hair and wrinkled hands
soft as feathers. In her backyard,
we feed birds bread. Pigeons so close
we could christen them. Wrens and warblers
congregate. Cindy drove me to church every Sunday
after my mother died. Before I leave
today, she'll make me recite the rosary in the parlor,
sunlight revealing new lines on her face.
We don't go to church anymore.
She doesn't travel well. Christmas and Easter—
the only times we step inside St. Mary's. *Make a wish*,
she says—a cardinal's just landed, red cap sharp
as the pope's hat. Cindy was Mother's
catechism sponsor. She remembers her voice. I can't.
This pecks at my head, so I tell her.
But I've never told her how I call
her my fairy white godmother, never admitted
I no longer believe. As always,
when we go inside, I light the votive candles.

OF WASP HUM AND CATACOMBS

Because my brother cooked
coke into crack, some baking soda,
water, a little of this, a little of that.

If I remove the plank from his eye,
I'll break my mother's back. Oh,
how I forget! Mix up and confuse.

That's okay. She can't walk anyway.
And here I am walking, no, swarming
because a friend said something

about mothers scraping off
their daughters' clits in Somalia. I wish
I had a twin sister, whose eyes itched

when mine itched, whose ears—
My limbs dance alone.
Is someone talking about me? I don't

talk to my brother on the phone. *Hello,*
you have a collect call from—Seneca
choked on bloodsmoke. I fear my bones

are lined with cancer. I'm not joking.
I'm not cooking. I'm walking home
from the grocery, arms full of brown bags.

I'M MY FATHER'S NAME

I'm the tangled Christmas tree lights he cursed,
the logs he split for six dollars an hour, his Thunderbird
and/or the gnats haloing his bottle's lips. I'm the heel
of the platforms he wore in '72, the cake-cutter Afro pick
he split that white boy's wig with, the glass dick
he smokes his crack from. I'm the perm kit, the false
teeth bubbling in the cup on the nightstand as he sleeps,
the record collection he sold for crack. I'm the luggage
his eyes carry, the pride seeped out of his lips
when death stood on his chest and left for a future visit.
I'm the smell of his breath: menthol cigarettes,
tooth rot, and biblical thoughts. I'm each purple scar
on his face, the dance hall he never got to open,
the hamburgers he smuggled to TV night in prison. I'm
the fire in his voice when he told his stepdad,
If you hit me again we're going to war. I'm the sawed-off
he shot into the front porch, the Dawn dishwashing liquid
he showered with, the latex glove he used to pull out
his shit when he was constipated. I am Little Douglas.
I am Locust Street, his street, the block he made pop
with junkies. I am the boy on the corner, waiting to yell, *Police!*

LOST SIDE OF LOSS

That rattling animal, the self, you left

inside your mother. Take
your eyes away from the soil.

Look at the birds worrying
the trees.

       Act as if someone
is rubbing your head, whispering

without face, without tongue.

There's a hole
in your pocket, a gold frame

around her photo.

         In suits, men carry away
her casket, her voice, your eyelids.

KEEPING IT REAL

is like damming a river with a toothpick,

like Afros dowsed in kerosene, like tattooing

"Suburban Life" across your stomach

or humping a pillow-top mattress. Keeping it real

is like smoking a cigarette, wearing a nicotine

patch, and chewing Nicorette, like waiting

for Ecstasy pills to hit. Keeping it real is nail clippings,

nose hairs, and Ornette Coleman's saxophone.

The real shit is crying as your Dad places the glock

from his pocket in your palm—

Don't be no girl, motherfucker, shoot, nigga, shoot.

THE FIRST TIME I SEE MY FATHER'S BLOOD CLEANED

Fried chicken and cigarettes
    in my backpack,

I stand at the door
    unable to cross

the threshold. As if
    that hospital floor

is ice too thin to bear
    any weight. I hear

your younger self caught beneath,
    knocking your fists

against the brittle cold,
    not strong enough to break

through, your gray-black skin
    a city at night. Still,

I'm at the door
    with the greasy chicken

and smokes you asked for,
    watching you bleed.

Blood rushing
    through tubes so fast

it seems not to move. Artificial
    kidney does work

yours won't. You don't see
    me. You shiver between death

and sleep. I place my bag down,
    try to give you my time,

the thing you wouldn't ask for,
    and didn't need, what

I'd been longing to give.

FISHING

I hear myself on voicemail, and I'm afraid.

Did time start the moment I began measuring it—
the way I was just a baby until I was named?
Once my tongue loosed words,
there was nothing to talk about. Hunting
and pecking, I found my way. The picture
on the wall is of me only because my mother
told me. I drag fingernails across my flesh.
Someone told me every seven years
we're brand new. If only we'd leave
skins like cicadas.
If I believed in Jesus, I'd ask to touch
the wounds. It's not me moving;
it's the dark. Black hides on both sides
of the mind. No one tells the maple leaves
to let go. I cannot catch the sun even though

I've wrapped it in a vowel and two consonants.

THIS POEM ISN'T BLACK

I am not myself. I am sleeping

      on the backseat of my brother's
white Jeep Cherokee.

           Crack

under the seat. Crack flooding
his blood.

Hard to tell memory from the real. I am trying,

trying to make this image tar,
but I don't wanna be leashed

to only reading this poem
on Martin Luther King Boulevard.

Brightness leaping
               from the Cherokee.

He always tells me,
You be acting white.

           Those words

skin me down to the white flesh.

VERTIGO

I tell you all the reasons we shouldn't be
together: (None of them involve race or the face
I gave you the first time I saw your parents' crib.)

my immeasurable desire,
my dreams of other women riding me,
the ebb and flow of daily routine

that could lull our love to sleep. You tell me
sober up, but my mind is clear
as Canyon Lake when our canoe

twirled us in circles as though the two of us
were one leaf spinning
with nothing beneath but wide sky.

GIVE ME MY MAMA BACK

I'm gonna kidnap Christ.
Give me a roll of duct tape
and a switchblade. I'm gonna
gash out his eyes, lash
his other side, finger his stigmata.
I'll cut myself, give up
a pound of flesh, slit Satan's wrists,
piss on his flames, lift dirt
from graves, unfasten the manacles
of slaves. With my tongue,
I will pick the lock
on death's door. All this to hear
her voice calling me home,
to see her eyes behind
those cat-eye frames, to feel
her cigarette breath against my neck
as she combs through my curls,
me between those thighs
that once spread wide,
so I could come into this world.
A joint hanging from her lips, she
tells me, *Boy, you know we gonna
get in some shit for this.*

WHOSE LITTLE BOY ARE YOU?

Too ornery to die,
                        while he coded blue,
my father saw us
arrive by helicopter,
my lover and me walking
on the hospital lawn.

Y'all looked just like the Obamas, except for Kay

being white, he said.
Before chest-shock rocked

his body back, he talked
to his mother, grandmother,
and my mother.
                        Call it
the Yalta Conference.
Peace made. Demarcations
drawn. I thought he'd be different.

Doctor said his brain
sat without oxygen
for a long time. *I know*

I was the one y'all asked about pulling the cord.

He doesn't remember dying,
only dreaming. *How kind
of the body*, I thought,

and wondered if that's the way
it always goes.

MY BROTHER SMOKED ROCKS WITH
A QUR'AN AT HIS FEET

When the man with the Nation of Islam
asks if I wanna buy a *Final Call*,

the burned plastic smell of crack
wafts into my nostrils, and I think

of Trey, my brother who bought me
Jordans and clothes two sizes too big,

the brother who taught me how to dribble
and play chess, pawns clasped

in his palms. Trey, the man everyone calls
Shabba Ali, the name he received in prison.

Trey who wasn't allowed to come
back home because of the rocks

in his pockets, the rocks he sold
on the corner of Fourteenth and Sycamore. Usually

Black Muslims ignore me
because of my white lover, but Kay isn't

with me today. Trey used to say:
You'll never catch me with a white woman.

Still, I grew an Afro just like him,
loved the Wu-Tang Clan,

tried to be left-handed.
The man senses my hesitation, offers

me incense: *Ten for a dollar.*
I see Trey in his polo and baggy khakis.

He always stomped me when we played chess
but never could outsmart the cops.

LOVE'S AUSTERE AND LONELY OFFICES

Said enough about dad, mom, and brother.
    What about my aunt, more mother
than the headstone I visit on Mother's Day?
    Movies, softball, and Bingo, her hobbies.

The coverall pays 1,000 dollars, enough
    for two months' rent. So often all she needs is O-64.
Who knows how much money she's spent?
    Dougie, get your mind out my purse! Don't

be counting my money, she'd say.
    Card games at our house. Cigarette smoke,
threaded gold letters on Crown Royal bags.
    Games of choice, Tonk or Spades.

That's my high. Jessie, you got the low.
    High yellow Miss Tammy had elbows darker
than shadows. *Girl, she know she need*
    some Vaseline. Didn't go to Bingo as much

as I should have. Her brother has all his Bingo cards
    memorized, more than two tables' worth—
I think of Malcolm X believing West Indian Archie
    would have been a great mathematician

if there was no Jim Crow. I think of the night
    I told her she didn't know enough about me
to love me. The way she told me I was a fool
    for not believing in God. *I'm sorry for all my sins*

with all my heart. She helped me memorize
  my prayers. Catholic school duties.
After her surgery, she told me,
  Dougie, now you'll always be my only baby.

NEVER LEFT MY NAME

in wet cement, haven't
observed Lent since high school.

Desert dust too much
like rust for forty

days. Ashes to frothed
tongue. Her mouth bruised

around her lips if
we kissed too long.

South Mountain, I rub
my skin to stone, felt

less and/or more alone.
Forgettable flesh. After

sex, I asked her to strip
every star from her

ceiling. She turned off
the lights to make it easier.

Her pinkie toes
had no nails.

WE HAD THE SECOND BIGGEST GYMNASIUM IN THE NATION

Razor blades for breakfast,
                washed down with aftershave.
Clean upper lip.
          Need something to stop me
from looking like my dad.
             Need something to stop
me from acting like my dad.
              Can't help but walk
the way he used to before
            his legs were amputated. Difficult to
swag-stroll on two prosthetics,
              but he tries, leans to the side
when he drives
          those electric wheelchairs at Wal-Mart.
Take him there,
          and I can end up anywhere:
Dougie, I got me a taste for a shake.
              Stop by Big Boy's.
Anderson is small enough
          to cross in fifteen minutes.
Trust me. I don't know
        how many times
I've done it.
         Rable Avenue to Columbus.
Riding by the high school.
          It's not Dad's, nor mine.
The three schools combined.
          What year? We don't remember.

Factories gone, too. Vacant lots,

                               dandelions working the cracks

in the cement. Windows

                      full of hairline fractures. Guide

Lamp and Delco Remy made this city

                           flush with greenbacks

long before crack made pockets

                    fat. I left town in 2004.

Never felt like home until I was walking

                        out the door.

TESTIFY

I swear on the melody of trumpet vines,
ants feasting through animal crackers, Burt's Bees,
Tyler Perry movies, my daddy's .38 slug, footie-socks
inside high-top Jordans, disidentification, drag
queens, blond dreadlocks, headstones
salt-and-peppering the grass, vanilla wafers
in banana pudding, Zeus-swan chasing,
blunt-guts, sharp thumbnails, keloid scars,
cash-only bars, R&B songs, on what the pot
called the kettle. I put that on my mama's good
hair, on playing solitaire with a phantom
limb, the white woman I go home to,
my auntie's face when she says: *You know*
he always loved them pink toes. I put that on
everything, on the signifiers I gobble up,
candlesticks blown out by whistling lips.
I put that on dervishing records scratched
on down-beats, empty beehives,
fresh-fade head-slaps, hand claps, bamboo shoots,
liminality, mestizos, the purple-black crook
of my arm, split sternums, on *You can't save*
him now. I put that on skinny jeans, get rich
quick schemes—*Gotta get that C.R.E.A.M. Know what*
I mean?—freckled black faces, leafless trees
throwing up gang signs, phlegm hocked
onto streets. I swear I catch more stones
than catfish. I lose more collard greens than sleep. I think
nothing is here but us darkies, high yellows, red bones,
cocoa butters. Someone, no, everyone has jungle fever.

Don't touch my forehead. Blond
as moonshine, mute trombone choking.
I put that on Instagram. Post me to the endless chain
of signifiers. Strawberry gashes on kneecaps, *Let me*
get some dap, Newports, Kool's, and folding
chairs instead of barstools, that white drool
caked on your face. *Mommy please wipe away*
the veil. I thought I was passing into the eye
of the streetlamp. I swear. I promise on frondless
palm trees, long pinkie nails, sixteen years, serve eight,
and Miss Addie's red beans and rice, Ol' Dirty Bastard
and the brother on the Cream of Wheat box. *It don't mean*
a thing if it don't buckle your knees. Open your hands.
I'll give you a song, give you the Holy Ghost
from a preacher's greasy palm—When he hit me, I didn't
fall, felt eyes jabbing me, tagging me. *Oh no he didn't!*—
give you the *om* from the small of her back.
I put that on double consciousness, multiple jeopardy,
and performativity. *Please make sure my fetters*
and manacles are tight. Yea baby, I like bottomless
bullet chambers. I swear on the creation of Uncle Tom—
some white woman's gospel. *She got blue eyes? I love*
me some—on Josiah Henson, the real Uncle Tom, on us still
believing in Uncle Tom. Lord, have mercy!
Put that on the black man standing on my shoulders holding
his balls. Put that on the black man I am—I am not—on
the black man I wish I was.

III

GOODNIGHT, BABY

I see Mother   naked

on the cooling board. Stopping

the incision, the mortician turns to me and says,   *Never forget.*

I am a boy   but know

how flesh stiffens, how

                    voices keep.

                    ——

Mound of dirt her body   makes

sleep to reach
sleep to

reach her hand

                    ——

Cemetery hills, red maple

red dogwood, red   bud tree, weeping

cherry. We're gas poured then   smoke.

———

Her   breasts, why do

I remember? Men

        in white ripped   the blouse from her chest.

———

If the sound

of the wind. If I don't

        smile at the Pacific,
                if I become stone.

———

I wore a choke-chain for   years, hoping

she would pull.

———

Jesus and myself high   above it all. God no

where like Mother. God no

where the day she   died. Here

but gone. Godless. Her not *Mama* or *Debbie*, now nameless. Now her

headstone. Her name written there. I read

it aloud. She won't

answer. It's Mother's Day, the air   thick. Wet

from her spit, from her mouth   yelling my name.

When I was born, she called me   *Baby*. The night

before she died, she said

              Good   *night, baby.*

———

She could read stones like faces.

———

She died at thirty-four.
I'm thirty-three.
        What used to be flakes off like dry skin.

CROWN HILL CEMETERY

It isn't the chessboard of stones,
the grass, the flags flailing in the heat,

the wigged birches with their thin
white arms and necks.

It's one headstone the size of a child,

white envelope to the right that says
From Mom placed next to the picture

of a boy born in 1983 like me. He's
clutching a yellow-eyed cat and hanging

above it all—staked, a headless
camouflage hat.

BULLETS AIN'T GOT NO NAMES ON THEM

Aim imprecise.

          Misses like language.

Watch out.

Those are bodies falling through the cracks.

Brother from 'round the way says, *They left
niggas leaking last night.*

          PoPo had the block

hot as a sauna. I see spray painted T-shirts.

I'm tired of RIP. I'm tired of TV. I'm tired
of shootings. He assures me,

          This Napghanistan, homie.

WHAT I WISH MY MOTHER
HAD TOLD MY FATHER

Tell your bitches
I'm coming out.
Tell 'em I'm gonna
wear my skirt,
that skirt that makes my ass
the apple of your eye,
that tight black mini
that turns heads, that skirt
I bought for myself
because you're a broke ass.
I'm gonna put on
my yellow heels,
the ones that let
my toes peek out.
I'm gonna run
the hot comb
through my hair.
Tell your bitches
my hair is too fine
for a perm. Tell 'em
they better back
the fuck off
the moment I walk
through the door
swinging my hips,
licking my lips, because
it's my bed you come
home to after
your small head spits

out all its bullshit.
Tell 'em I'm the one
with the bail money,
the rent money, the light
money, the food money. *Shit!*
All the money! Tell your bitches
I'm coming out tonight.

I CAN RUN FIVE MILES BUT CAN'T GET TO THE OTHER SIDE OF MY MIND

Always been the type to hold a hornet

in my fist—numb is another word

                              for fed up. I pull

nose hairs to cry. Love, to me,
is the vine strangling the locust tree. Tell me

to take a stand. I'll have a seat.
Show me heaven's cliffs. I'll leap.

                              I'm a June bug,
and it's September.

My lips hate one another, so I can't shut up.

IS THAT MY FATHER?

At the hospital, I rub his heel with oil, saving
some for that knob that was once his full leg.

The blinds slice a streetlamp's light into stripes
above his nappy hair. IV tubes and cords

writhe around his bed. His mouth circled with froth.
In the morning as I drive out of the parking lot

and head toward Highway 65, light sweeps
into the empty passenger seat, the place where he

would be sitting if I didn't have to leave him, if
he wasn't dying. In a cornfield, he struts

on two legs, wearing suspenders and a white bowtie,
his right arm loose, swinging time. He smiles,

spins in place, his hair relaxed, black,
and flat. Glistened to shine by golden stalks and sun,

anointed and crowned—*I'm a bad man*,
he yells to me, both of us annihilated by all that light.

I'M SUSPICIOUS

if it fits, if it exists.

Chiseled, our ways.

Me, for instance,
always chewing the end

of my pen. I like
ink blue, the hue
of the seventh note. Sound

more tangible. I am
against easy,
in the pocket, right

where voices meet. Give me discordance

and a Forty of Mickey's.
Punch the sundial. Pile

your kitty litter dreams.
Reach in. Dig, fool, dig.

Dust had enough.

Put some stank on it. Let's
drink to what
remains unlocked. Not
the key, holed for chain,

round body thinning
to jagged teeth.
Not the open—

the shut is what I
want shut.

ALL IS LAUGHTER

A dance of fists—I wasn't
there, but people say you were

too drunk. Wind would
have toppled you if his punches

hadn't, but you fought anyway,
swung wide and wild, landed

only a couple blows, while his
fist struck sixteenth notes

on your face. You staggering
up. Him telling you to stay

down. I am sitting on your lap.
I am your little brother. I am

younger than I am now. We are
eating ice cubes. You tell me

you love the sound of knuckle
to skull, the look a face gives

before a man falls. Making
my hand a fist, you place it

on your jaw, buck your eyes
and push my small clenched hand

into your mandible. You tumble
us to the floor.

KNEE DEEP

Father wants to be buried in a pinstripe suit,
        says give him a money clip full of loot and the Funkadelic
record, *Uncle Jam Wants You.* Me, I imagine cremation:

ashes released at Joshua Tree or into the Pacific. Cliché,
        I've thought, so now opt for the plot beside my mother:
maybe we'll talk, maybe our voices will mix into a stew,

bone-mash and echoing-shadow. Wouldn't care how
        they dressed me as long as I was cleaned and touched
with love before I was put away to rot. I think more

people should get massages. Face down in the nude,
        somebody pushing love into you. *Not a luxury,*
the receptionist at Massage Envy says, *a necessity.* Probably

not, but I bought a membership. Buried alongside my mother,
        grandma, grandpa, uncles, and aunts: a clan of us. Admission?
Blood, family squabbles, awkward kisses. *One cheek*

or two? Dare for the lips? I never asked Dad if he wanted to be
        buried with his prosthetic legs. Surely, he'd need them.
Surely, they'd be fastened secure when he got up to rise.

PRAY TO THIS

1.

Wet memory of my dead
mother's voice, a soaked
    residue. What

I remember is fluxed before
the fall off the cliff: no
    splash, clash, or clang

ringing off the rounded gong
of gone. The difference
    between *I think it was*

and *I don't recall*,
too slick. Her voice on the tip
    of my tongue, then snatched.

2.

Don't let the streetlights catch you,
        Mama says before I leave.

Tall poles with glaring bulbs,
        their limbs could grab me,

take me into some deeper night. It isn't
        shining beams she fears.

Don't let—hooded figures—
        the streetlights—who spark

guns—*catch you*—specters selling
        white rocks. Flames

I can't see. She can
        but can't know

her body will quit—*Don't let*
        the streetlights catch you—can't

know those red and blue lights
        taking away Dad,

brother, and her body too.

3.

I hold on to the priest's words
floating on dark, needing
the calm of his homily.
I see that small boy with the hi-top
fade, the one who wore
those itchy slacks his mother bought.
Her favorite song: "On Eagle's Wings."
He doesn't know why. Inside
this church today a woman
with white hair sings that song,
Mama's song. Mama's rising.
I rise, step into the Communion line.
Mama's singing. I sing. The priest
lays bread on my tongue. *Body
of Christ.* I say, *Amen.* Red wine
warms my head. I say, *Amen.*

4.

Your mama gonna send me to the penitentiary, Dad says.

The lawn bathed in milklight, his face straight and solemn,

eyes cold as the moon as he shows where

her fingernails dug craters into his cheeks. Still

in half-sleep, I see bees and flies sharing sky. Knuckles

swollen, he slips from his belt loop a gun,

hands it over. Its metallic barrel throws a rainbow

across my face. The pistol, heavier than a full milk jug.

5.

Mama's not in this picture, already

dead in August. It's my First
Communion. Father Bob's there.
My father stands behind him

on a step, a shadow. His black
shades hide his eyes.

His mustache touches his nostrils
the way mine does now.

Is he high?

6.

Mama's still

        plaiting rows in my hair,

one strand over another, crisscrossing
down the nape.

        The lanyard-curls warm,

a coiled snake.
She rubs grease

into my scalp, cooling the pull,
the tear of hair, the smell

        of olive oil.

Then ash, her fingers, her hands, her

face blown away.

7.

Background red.
Mama, Grandma, where are y'all?

Both dressed in black,
Grandma with her fedora cap, purse

in her lap—I only remember
her Pall Malls. There must be

a pack in her purse. Mama's standing
next to her, must be before

multiple sclerosis, before her mind let go
of her legs. She wears a tie, a skirt

to her ankles. Dark stockings hide
her light skin. Grandma sits

in a wicker chair, Huey P. Newton–style
but without the rifle and spear.

Mama's hair's curled. She had to sleep
in rollers to make it stay.

8.

Boy perches on top a ladder,

below a swirl of umbral-pull and light-push,

his brother hot-boying: coke, baking

soda, and water boiling in a pot, his father

flaming a white rock. His mother

tries to wiggle her toes, can't, and stops.

9.

All and nothing sacred.
        Skin more   nothing more

than cloak   body taut
        ripped from thought.

Somewhere in the thick of gone,
        what waits   to show me what

I forgot, what

I let drop?

THE CRIPPLE AND THE CRACKHEAD

If there is a way, a proper way, to lift
your damp, naked ex-wife

out of the bathtub, he guesses this is it,
folding one crack-slackened arm under

her legs, the other above the small of her back.
Once there were women with ice-pick eyes

and sin-grins, the ones he fucked
while she slept in their bed alone. But now

he's here. Crack somersaults in his veins,
but he is here, her wet, black hair

dripping on the back of his hand. The sound
of this moment not the blues, not a plea, a testimony:

her lips touch his cheek as he carries her.
This instant wide and round—

their son's eyes when he sees that kiss.

NOTES

LOUD LOOKS

"Luke Perry." American actor who starred as Dylan McKay on the TV series *Beverly Hills, 90210* from 1990 to 1995, and again from 1998 to 2000.

"Tom Petty." American musician, singer, songwriter, multi-instrumentalist, and record producer.

"You Don't Know How It Feels." The lead single from Tom Petty's 1994 album *Wildflowers*.

"All black people are fluent in silence." A friend said it in class one day, but I don't think James Baldwin ever said this. I looked many places for this quotation and could never find it. I hope he said it though.

AUBADE

"Circle, circle, dot, dot. Nobody gave me a shot . . ." A play on the American children's playground song, "Circle, circle, dot, dot. Now you got your cootie shot."

FEELS LIKE RAIN

"Big Wheel." Children's tricycle.

ENTREATIES

"2g." Slang for the year 2000.

"Five-Percent." Short for the Five-Percent Nation, an organization created by Clarence Smith in Harlem, New York in 1964. Smith (Clarence 13X) was a former member of the Nation of Islam.

"With a loud voice I cry out to the Lord; with a loud voice I beseech the Lord. My complaint I pour out before him." (Psalms 142:2-3).

ME, *THE BOONDOCKS.* HER, *SOUTH PARK.*

"The Boondocks." American adult animated sitcom on Cartoon Network's

late-night programming block, Adult Swim. The sitcom was created by Aaron McGruder and was based off his comic strip with the same name.

"South Park." American adult animated sitcom created by Trey Parker and Matt Stone for the Comedy Central television network.

"Token." The name of one of the only black characters on the show *South Park*.

"Uncle Ruckus." The name of a character on *The Boondocks*. He is black but hates black people.

"Def Comedy Jam." A HBO television series produced by Russell Simmons.

"The medium is the message." is a phrase coined by Marshall McLuhan.

"All that is to come is vanity." (Ecclesiastes 11:8).

"Elijah Muhammad." Black religious leader who led the Nation of Islam from 1934 until his death in 1975.

"James Baldwin." Black novelist, essayist, playwright, poet, and social critic.

INDEFENSIBLE

"Dear Mama." The lead single from 2Pac's third studio album *Me Against the World*.

"Brenda's Got a Baby." A single from 2Pac's debut album *2Pacalypse Now*.

"All Eyez on Me." The name of the fourth studio album by 2Pac.

"All Bout U." The second track on the first disc of the 2Pac album *All Eyez on Me*.

"Wonda Why They Call U Bitch." The fourth track on the second disc of the 2Pac album *All Eyez on Me*.

"Brown Skin Lady." The sixth track on Black Star's album *Mos Def & Talib Kweli Are Black Star*.

MIC DROP

"Mounds State Park." State park in Anderson, Indiana.

"ARE YOU READY TO HELP THE PARENTS OF THIS CHILD IN THEIR DUTY AS CHRISTIAN PARENTS?"

"Are you ready to help the parents of this child in their duty as Christian parents?" These words are part of the Rite of Baptism for children in the Catholic Church.

OF WASP HUM AND CATACOMBS

"Seneca." Referring to Seneca the Younger (Lucius Annaeus Seneca).

KEEPING IT REAL

"Ornette Coleman." American jazz saxophonist, violinist, trumpeter, and composer. He was a major contributor to the free jazz movement of the 1960s.

VERTIGO

"Canyon Lake." One of four reservoirs that were formed by the damming of the Salt River in Arizona.

WHOSE LITTLE BOY ARE YOU?

"Whose little boy are you?" A question from James Baldwin's 1963 book *The Fire Next Time.*

MY BROTHER SMOKED ROCKS WITH A QUR'AN AT HIS FEET

"*Final Call.*" The official newspaper of the Nation of Islam founded in 1979 by Minister Louis Farrakhan.

"Wu-Tang Clan." American hip hop group from New York City.

LOVE'S AUSTERE AND LONELY OFFICES

"Love's austere and lonely offices." Part of the line from Robert Hayden's poem "Those Winter Sundays."

"Tonk." A matching card game, which combines features of knock rummy and conquian.

"**Spades.**" A trick-taking card game created in the 1930s.

"**West Indian Archie.**" A Harlem gangster in *The Autobiography of Malcolm X*.

WE HAD THE SECOND LARGEST GYMNASIUM IN THE NATION

"**We Had the Second Largest Gymnasium in the Nation.**" The gymnasium was called the Anderson High School Wigwam. It opened in 1961 and was closed in 2011. At maximum capacity, it could hold 8,996 people.

"**Guide Lamp.**" An Anderson, Indiana automotive headlight factory that was part of the Guide Corporation. The company was founded in 1906 and went out of business in 2007.

"**Delco Remy.**" An Anderson, Indiana factory that closed in 1994. The company is now a part of the Remy International, Inc. and is headquartered in Pendleton, Indiana.

TESTIFY

"**Burt's Bees.**" Lip balm products from the American personal care company that is a subsidiary of Clorox.

"**C.R.E.A.M.**" An acronym and song (the eighth track on the album *Enter the Wu-Tang*) created by the Wu-Tang Clan that means "Cash Rules Everything Around Me."

"**Ol' Dirty Bastard.**" Russell Tyrone Jones, an American rapper and producer. He was one of the founding members of the Wu-Tang Clan.

"**Josiah Henson.**" Author, abolitionist, and minister who wrote *The Life of Josiah Henson, Formerly a slave, Now an Inhabitant of Canada, as Narrated by Himself* (1849), a text that is believed to have inspired Harriet Beecher Stowe's *Uncle Tom's Cabin*.

CROWN HILL CEMETERY

"**Crown Hill Cemetery.**" A cemetery located in Indianapolis, Indiana. It is the third largest non-governmental cemetery in the US.

KNEE DEEP

"Funkadelic." American funk band led by George Clinton.

"Uncle Jam Wants You." The eleventh studio album by American funk band Funkadelic.

"Joshua Tree." Joshua Tree National Park is located in southeastern California. It is named for the Joshua Trees (Yucca brevifolia) native to the park.

PRAY TO THIS

"On Eagle's Wings." A devotional song composed by Michael Joncas. Its lyrics are based on Psalm 91 and Isaiah 40:31.

"Huey P. Newton–style." Huey P. Newton was a political activist and revolutionary who, along with Bobby Seale, co-founded the Black Panther Party in 1966. Photos of him sitting in a wicker chair carrying a rifle and spear are now iconic.

"Hot-boying." is selling drugs and/or committing other crimes in a showy manner that attracts the attention of the police. This term was probably used first by The Hot Boys, an American rap group (1997–2001) from New Orleans, Louisiana that comprised the members Juvenile, Lil Wayne, B.G., and Turk.

GRATITUDES

When I was a child, I always told adults I wanted to be an author. I eventually grew out of that wide-eyed dream and moved on to wanting more practical professions: architecture, physical therapy, law. When those dreams fell asleep, I wanted to be a marine biologist, a high school basketball coach, a community organizer. Yet, the page kept calling me. My journals kept filling up. Remembering all of these dreams makes me especially thankful for Kate Gale and everyone at Red Hen Press (Much love and respect due to Rebecca Baumann, my tremendous publicist, Keaton Maddox, my sharp-eyed editor, and Selena Trager, my understanding production manager!) for helping me to fulfill my first dream, my most dear dream, the dream which feels the most mine, my dream of being an author. Kate Gale changed my life when she accepted my manuscript. To her I give my utmost gratitude and respect.

In addition, much respect and thanks due to David St. John, my beknighted OG, and Anna Journey for helping me to hone my voice into my song. I am also deeply indebted to Susan McCabe, my kindred spirit in mysticism and loyal listener. Without her my scholarly pursuits at the University of Southern California would be lost at sea. Thank you so much, Susan! Many thanks to Mark Irwin, a man who hears me when I can't hear myself and always helps my little poems find their ways. Thank you, my dear mentors. Each and every classmate and colleague at USC (Shout out and big ups to Michelle Brittan Rosado, Catherine Theis, Robin Coste Lewis, Diana Arterian, and Elise Suklje Martin to name a few!) deserves my gratitude as well. Thank you, my friends, for being the willing and discerning audience my writing needs. And I cannot forget to thank Janalynn Bliss for helping me trans-navigate my journey at USC. She is the lodestar to which I always look when I can't find my way.

Likewise, I cannot thank Alessandra Lynch enough for injecting my writing and psyche with her joyous music and shrewd guidance. I will forever be thankful for the afternoons under shaded tree when she taught me the art of revision with the weighted oomph of real re-imagining. And Chris Forhan looking at me with his eyes ever so slightly above the frames of his glasses, thank you, my sage, for teaching me prosody and for writing that amazing poem, "The Fidgeting." I return to that poem very often, homie. Its quiet mediations console me, make me feel less alone, and dare I say more whole? My time at Butler University was brightened by these two incredible poets and the indomitable Susan Sutherlin from whom I learned professionalism, tenderness, and acquired a penchant for Modernism. I still remember us debating whether Postmodernism even exists, a thought exercise I still play with students and friends. A special thanks must also be given to Hilene Flanzbaum for opening the world of literary theory for me. Without her tutelage, I would have never dreamed of applying to a PhD program. Thank you so much for helping me study for the English Literature GRE. And Andy Levy thank you for calling me that early spring afternoon and telling me of my acceptance to Butler. I will never forget that day. Was that the day I became a "real poet"? All of these people made Butler a home I miss more than daily. Thank you, friends!

My time at the Tin House Writer's Workshop was also very fruitful, so I would be remiss if I didn't send my thanks to my group leader Kevin Young and all my workshop mates there. The Napa Valley Writers' Conference was equally amazing. Many thanks to Camille Dungy for treating me seriously as a poet and for taking the time to engage with my work so thoroughly. I am beyond appreciative for that.

This piece would be more than a little bit incomplete if I did not also take a moment to thank Robert Haynes, my first mentor at ASU, for convincing me I could be a poet and for showing me a way to make a life out of a love of poetry and literature. He saw past my directionless cliché persona and helped me see the me I am now. Thank you, Bob. Thank you so very much. Back in my Arizona days Sarah Vap was also a guide. With her capacious wit and gentle voice, she taught me that it is all right for things to mean more than one thing at one time, a lesson I am still trying to fully comprehend, be comfortable with, and utilize. Thank you.

And finally, I would like to thank my family. Thank you Aunt Yvette for raising me and always making me feel like a blessing instead of a burden. Thank you Dad for teaching me what hard love looks like and feels like, for teaching me a lesson I am still working on: how to forgive myself and others. Thank you Derek (Big Cuzzo) for being my second father and big brother. Thank you Sandy and Bill for being the best Godparents ever. Thank you Kay for always believing, for never leaving, and for each and every long evening spent enjoying each other's thoughts. Thank you for being the anchor with which I moor myself.

BIOGRAPHICAL NOTE

Douglas Manuel was born in Anderson, Indiana. He received a BA in Creative Writing from Arizona State University and an MFA from Butler University where he was the Managing Editor of *Booth: A Journal*. He is currently a Middleton and Dornsife Fellow at the University of Southern California where he is pursuing a PhD in Literature and Creative Writing. He was a recipient of the Chris McCarthy Scholarship for the Napa Valley Writers' Conference and has been the Poetry Editor for Gold Line Press as well as was one of the Managing Editors of Ricochet Editions. His poems have appeared or are forthcoming in *Rhino, North American Review, The Chattahoochee Review, New Orleans Review, Crab Creek Review, Many Mountains Moving* and elsewhere.

www.douglasmanuelpoetry.com